Beach Bunnies

Hot Sexy Swimsuit Girls Models Pictures

By **PHOTO ART LOVER**

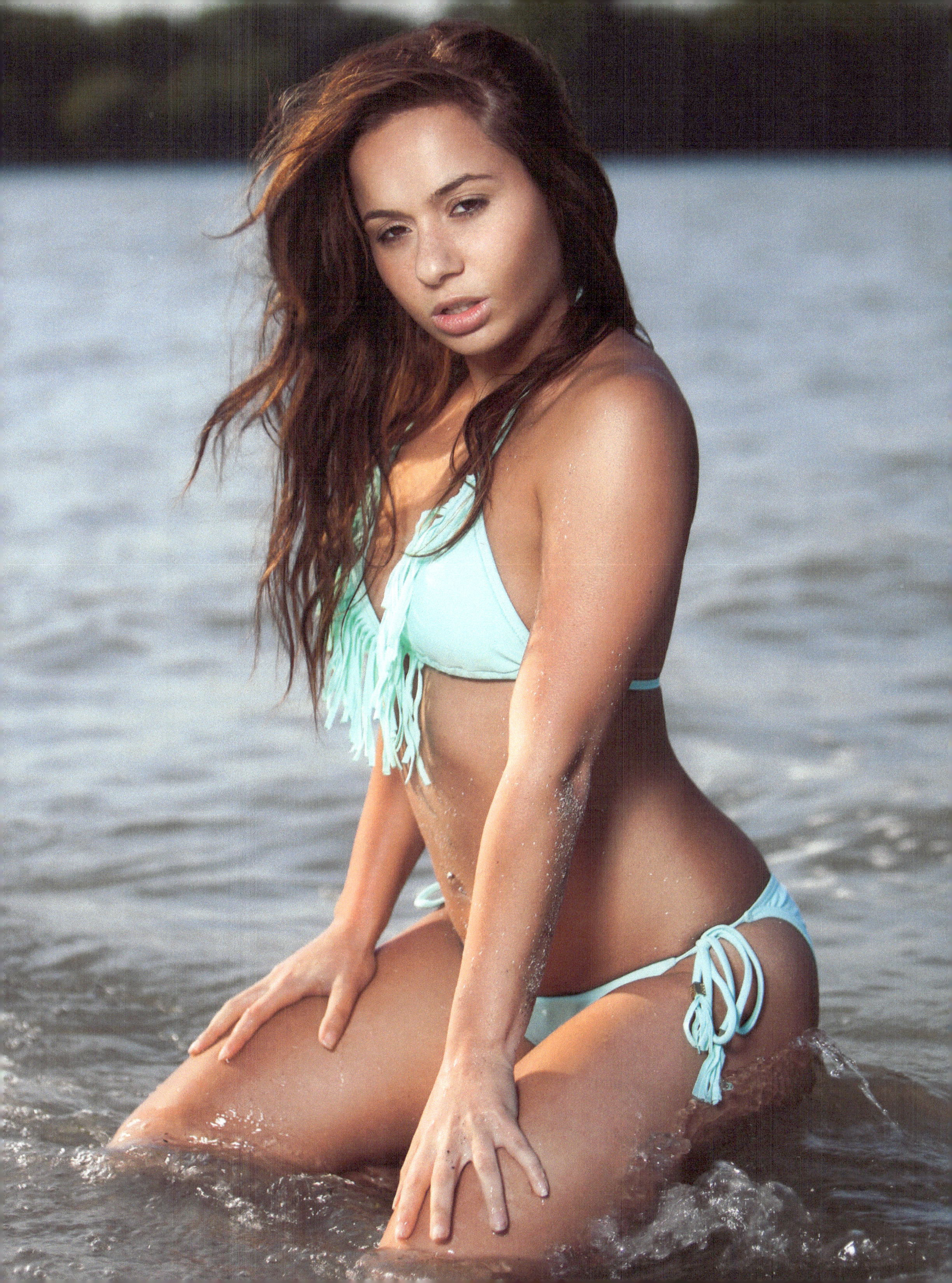

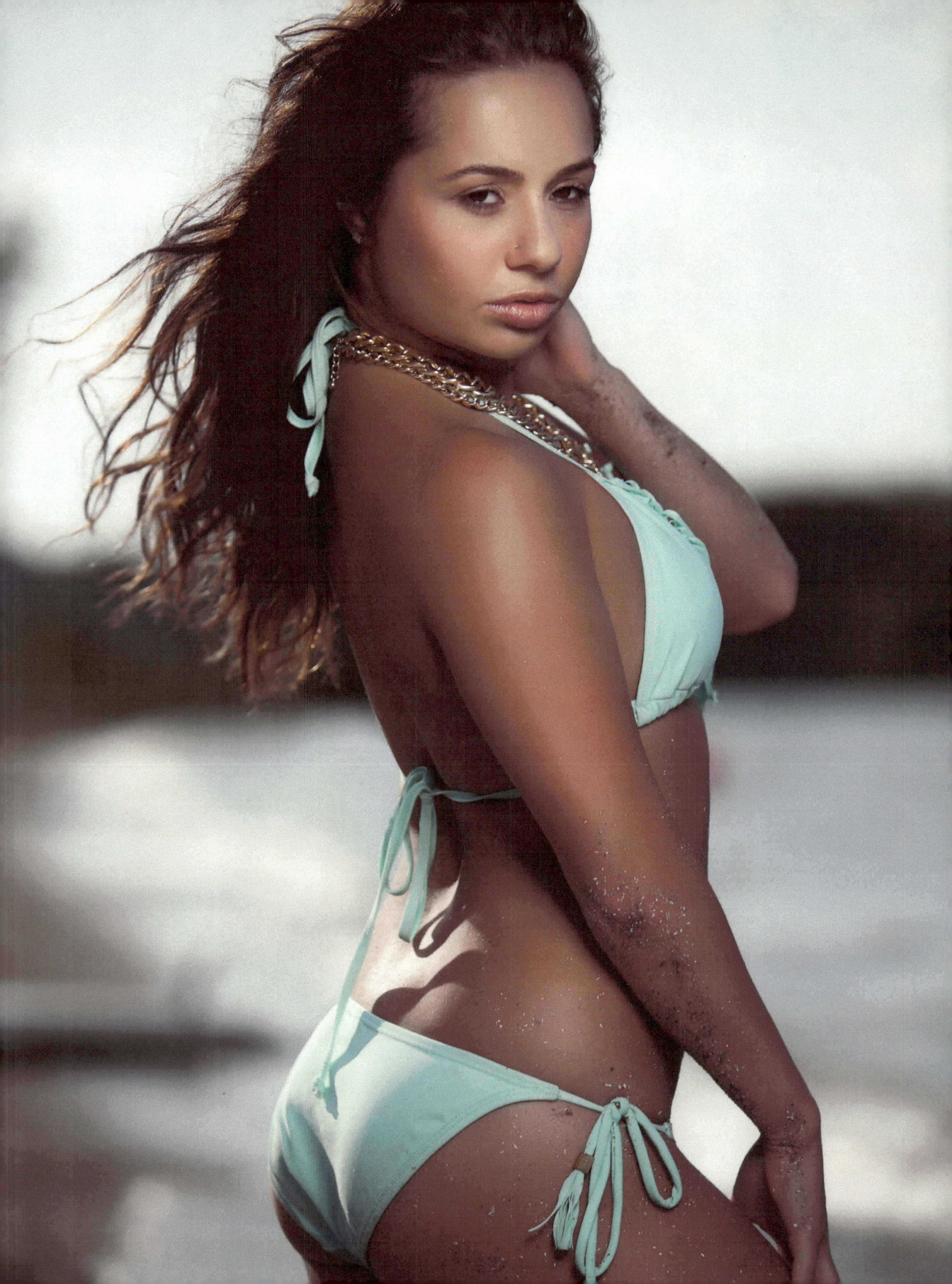

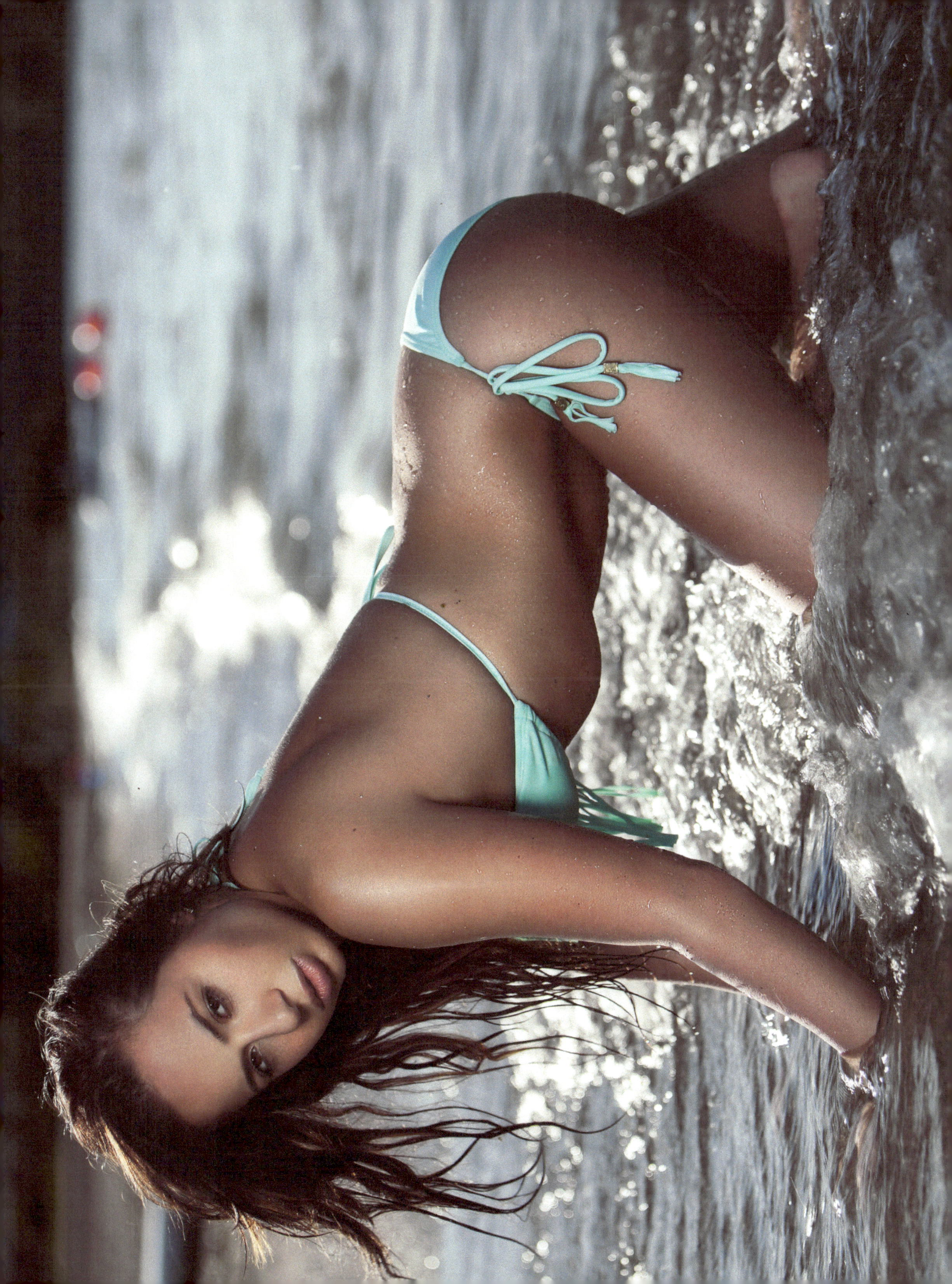

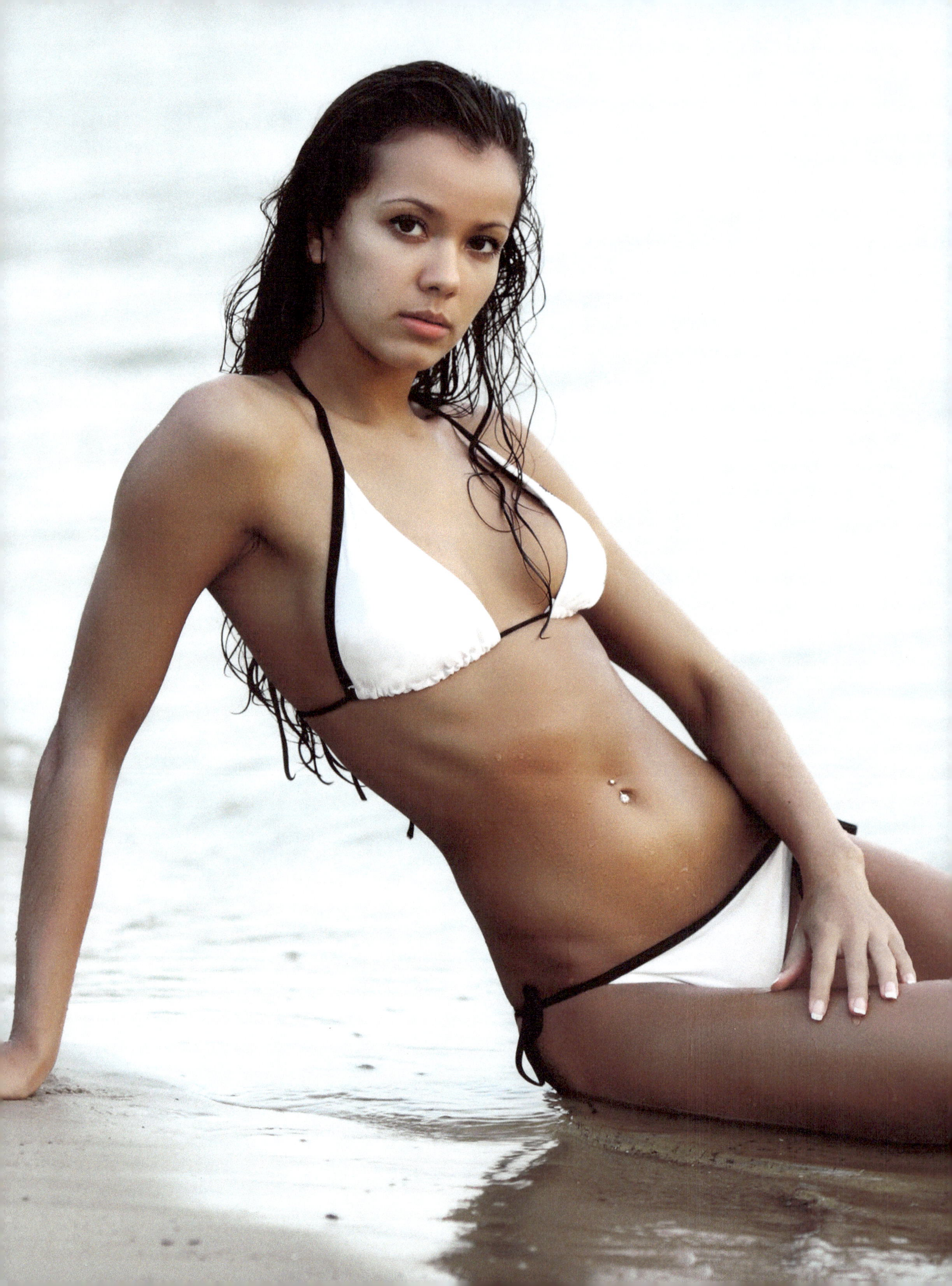

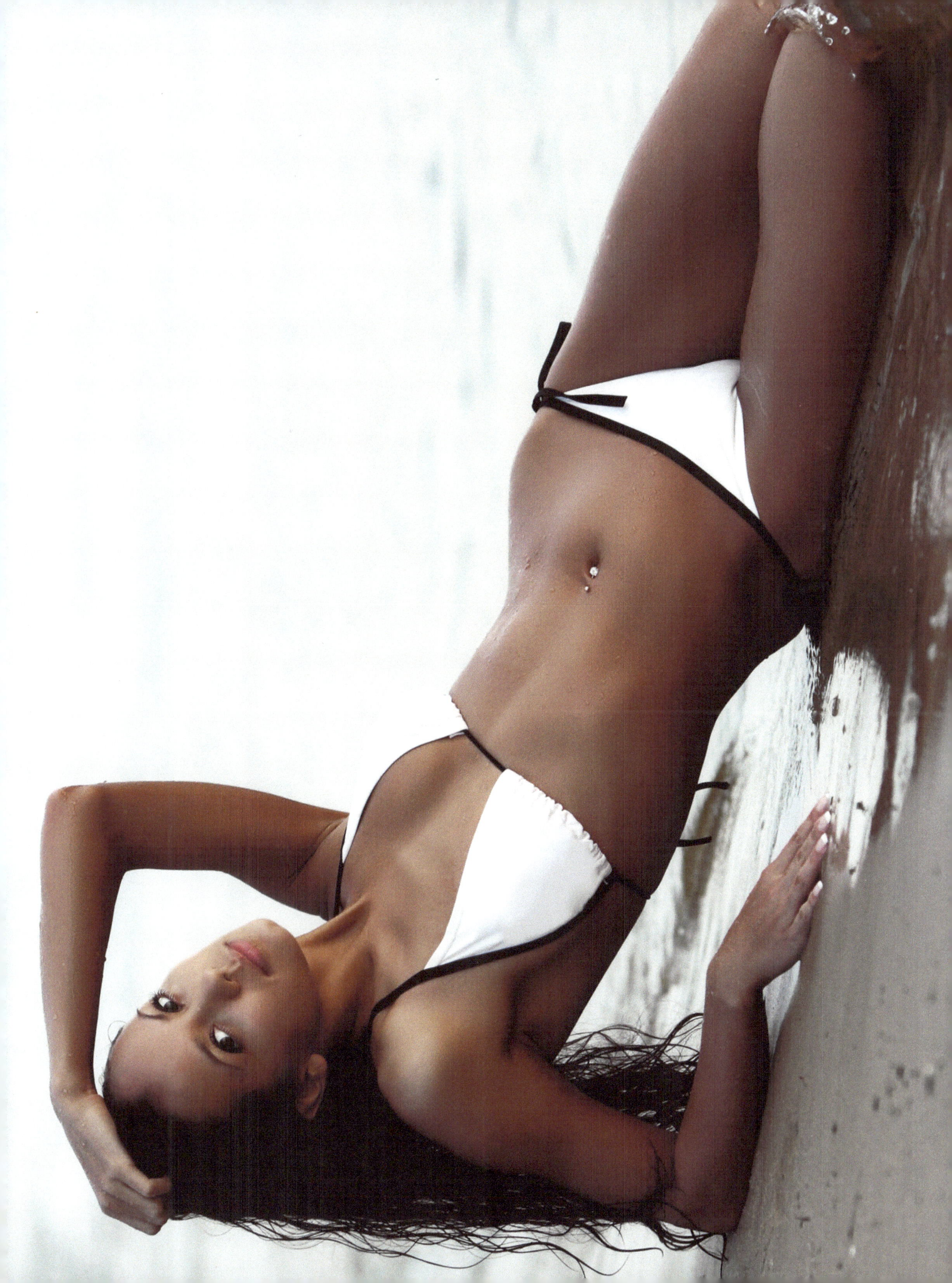

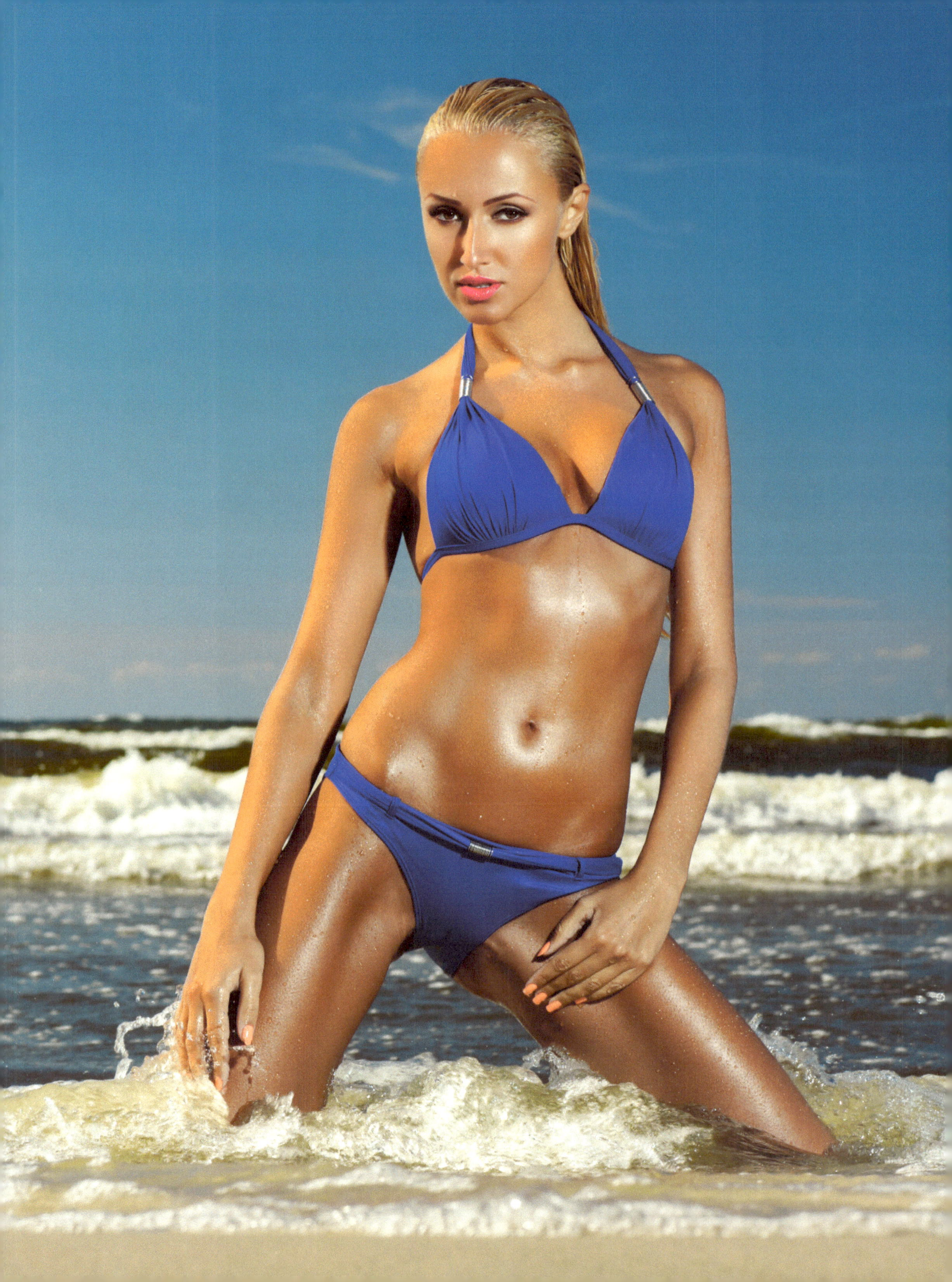

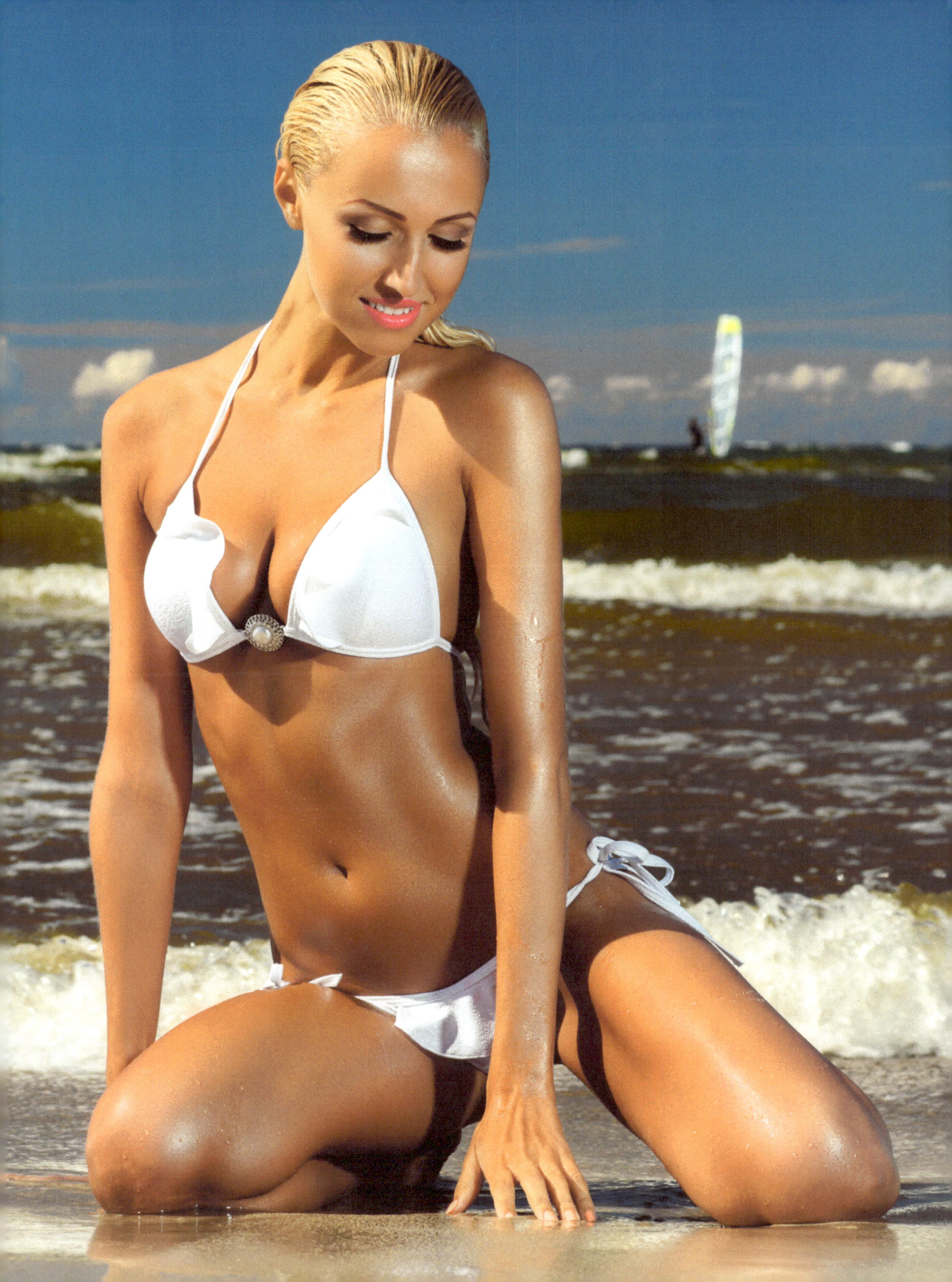

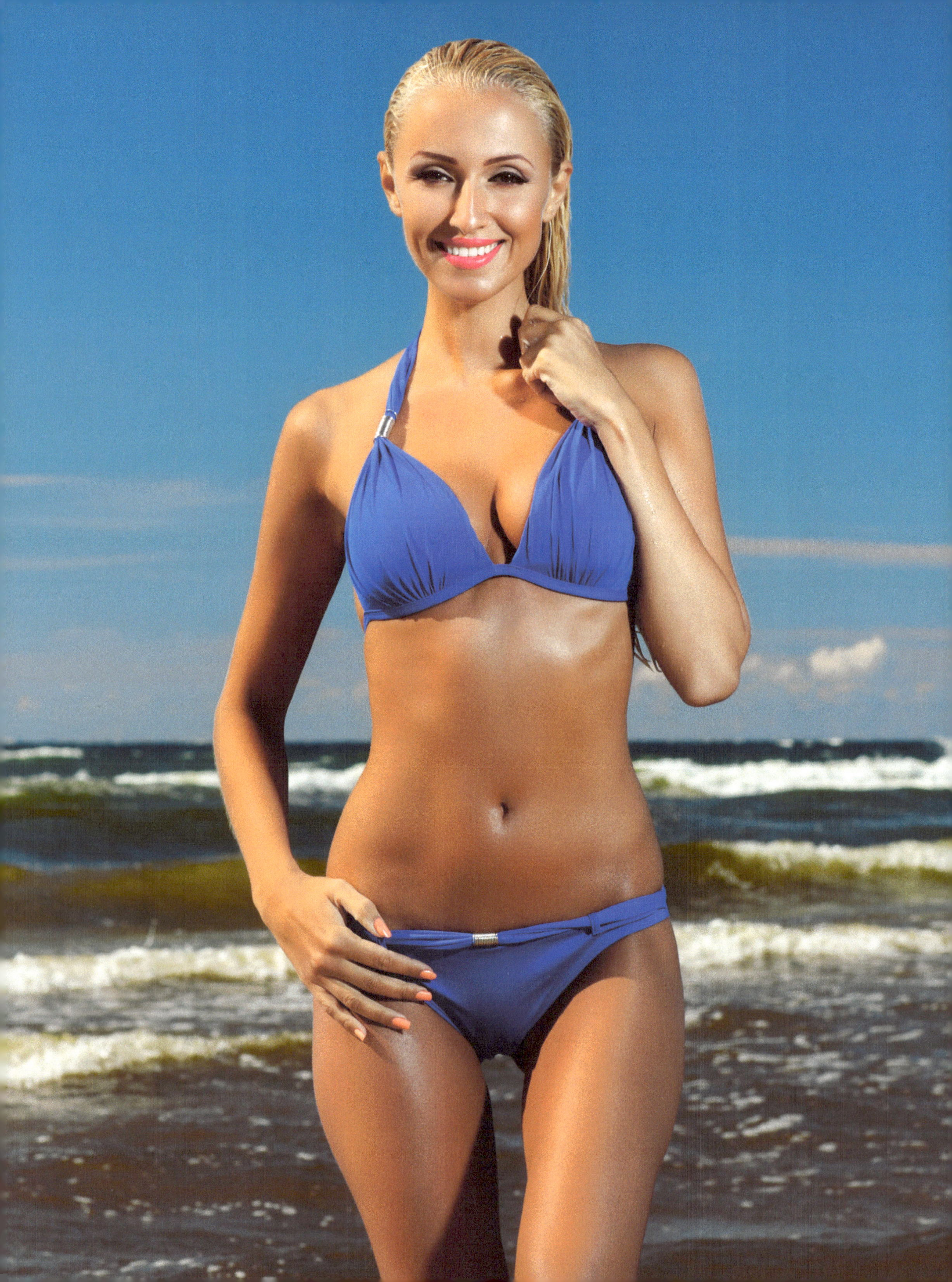

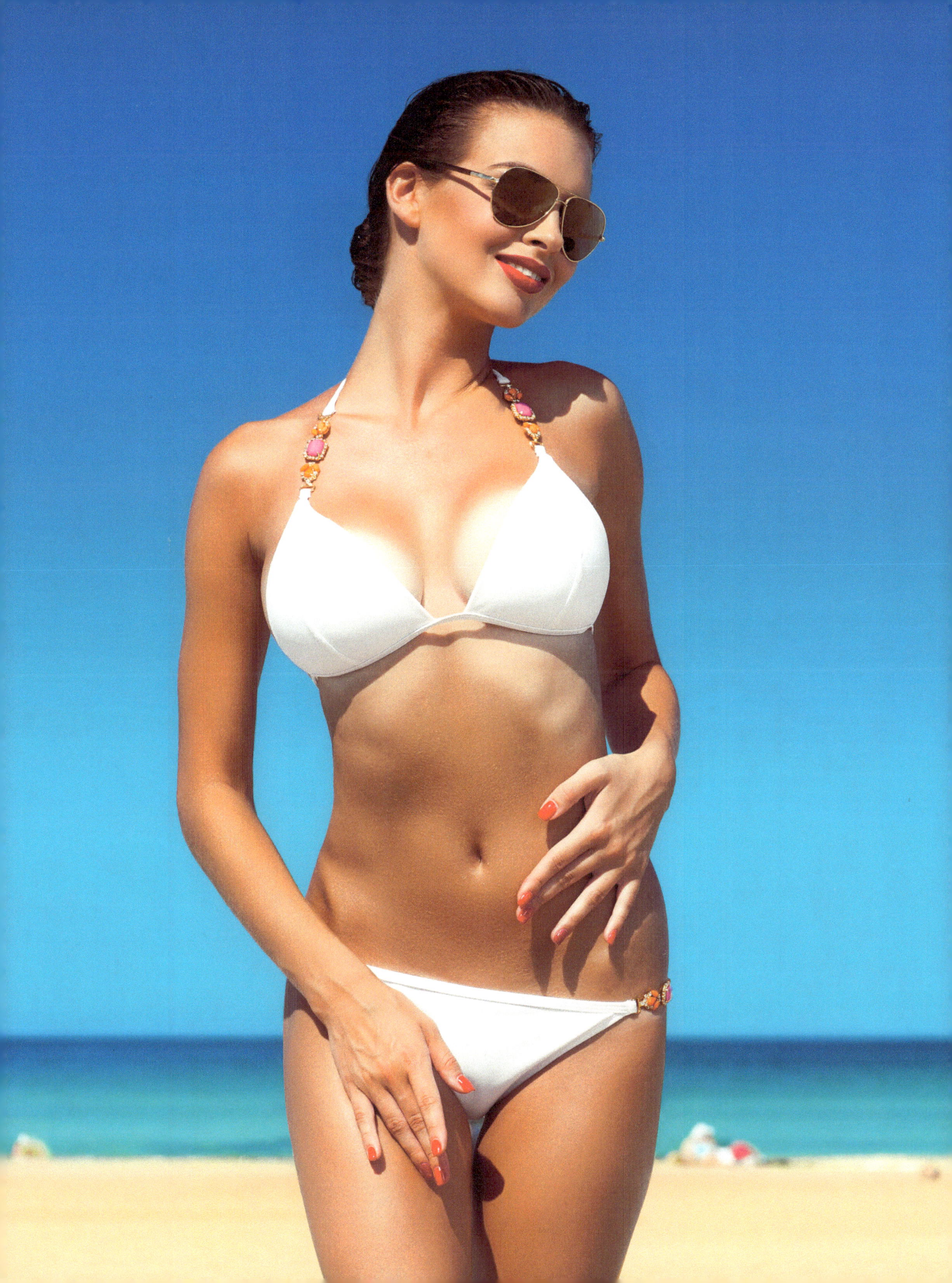

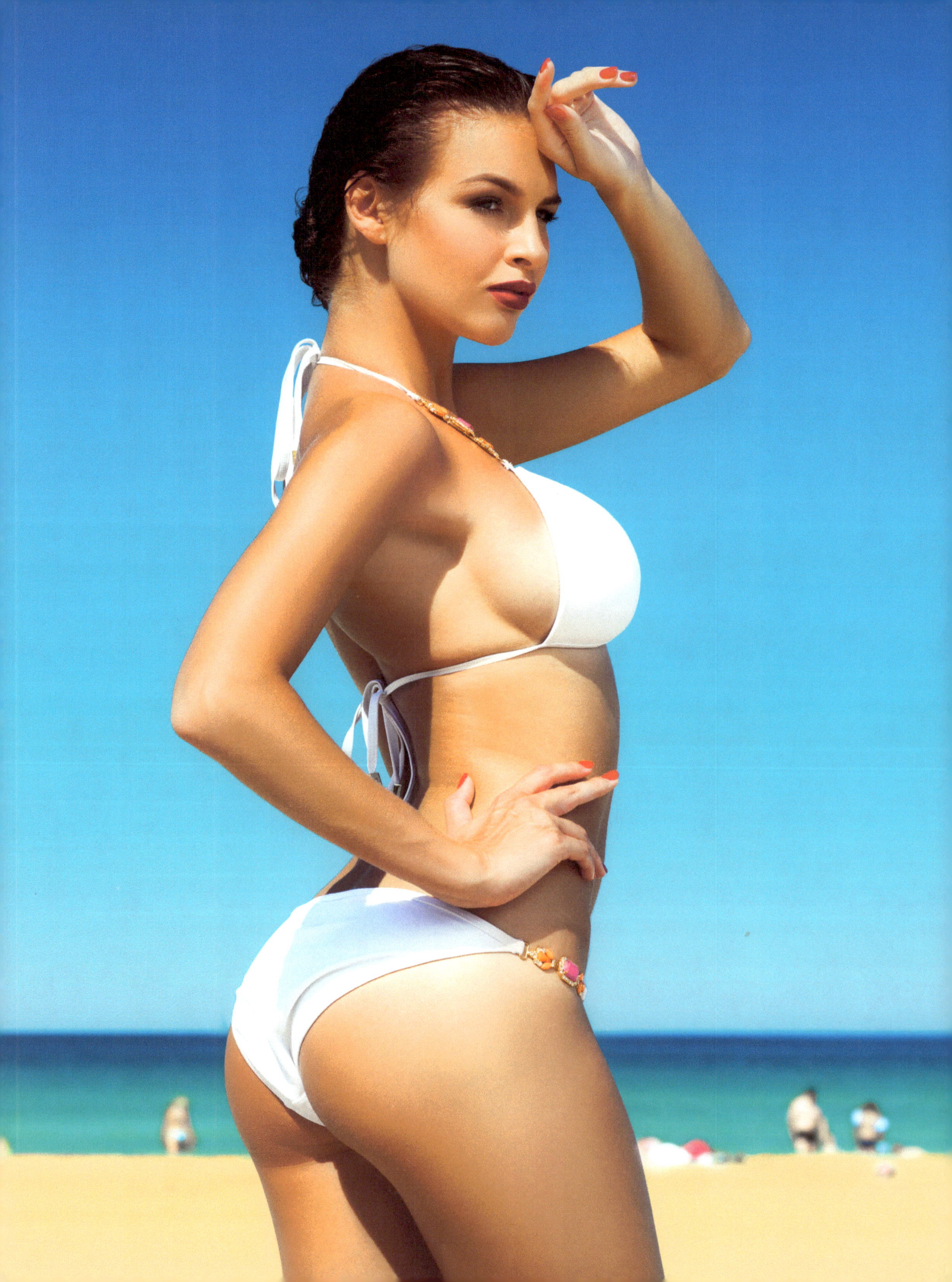

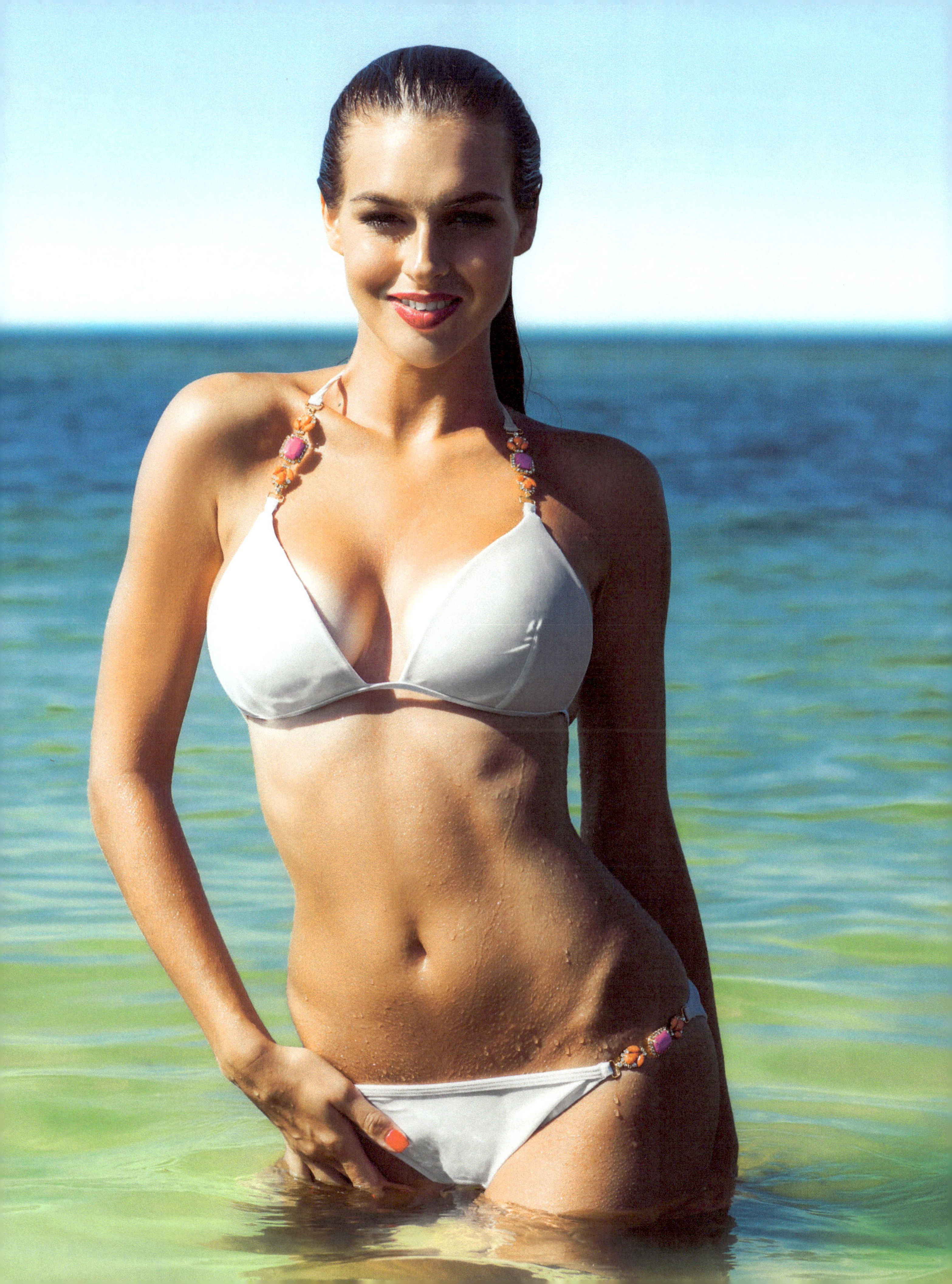

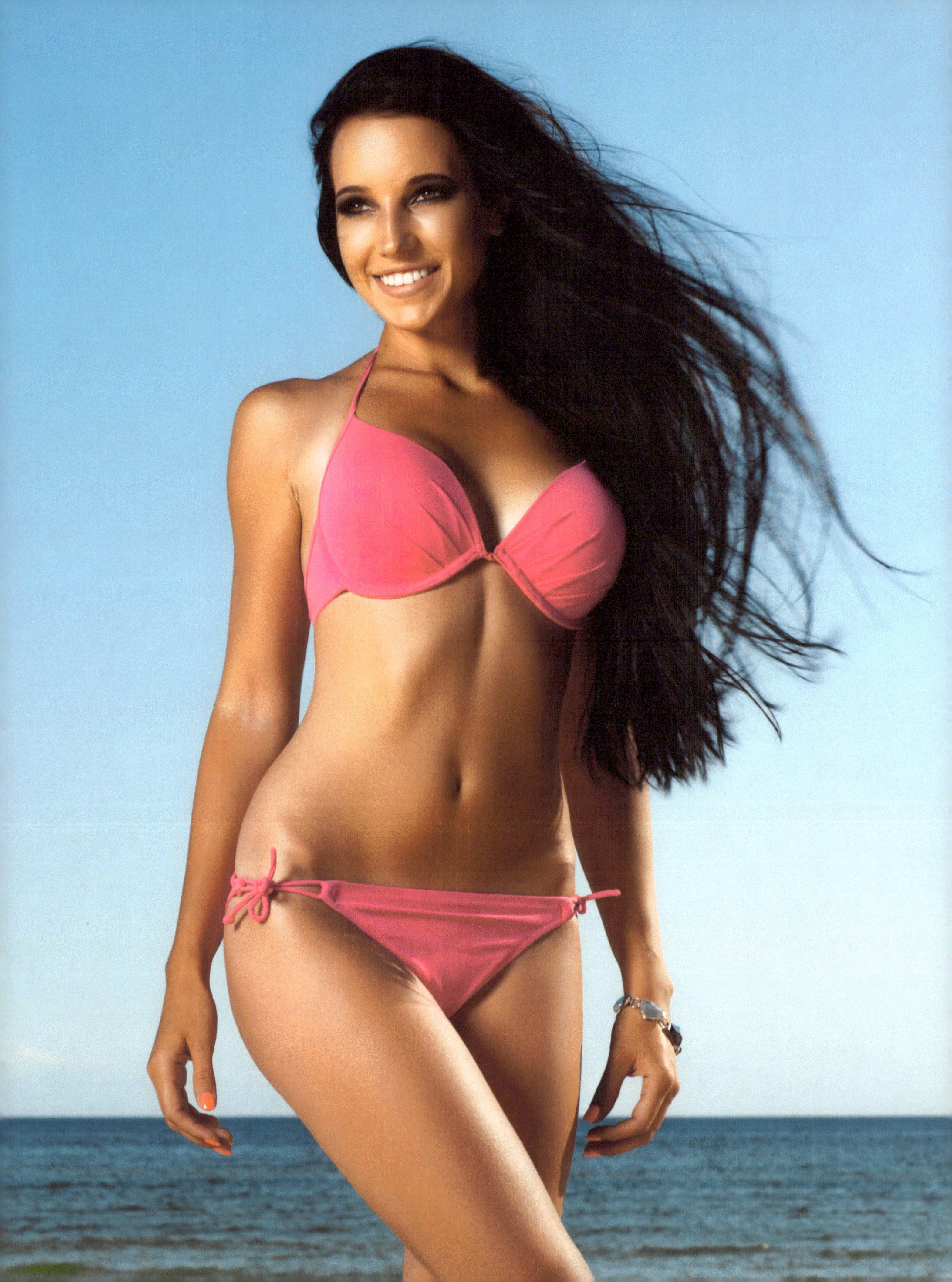

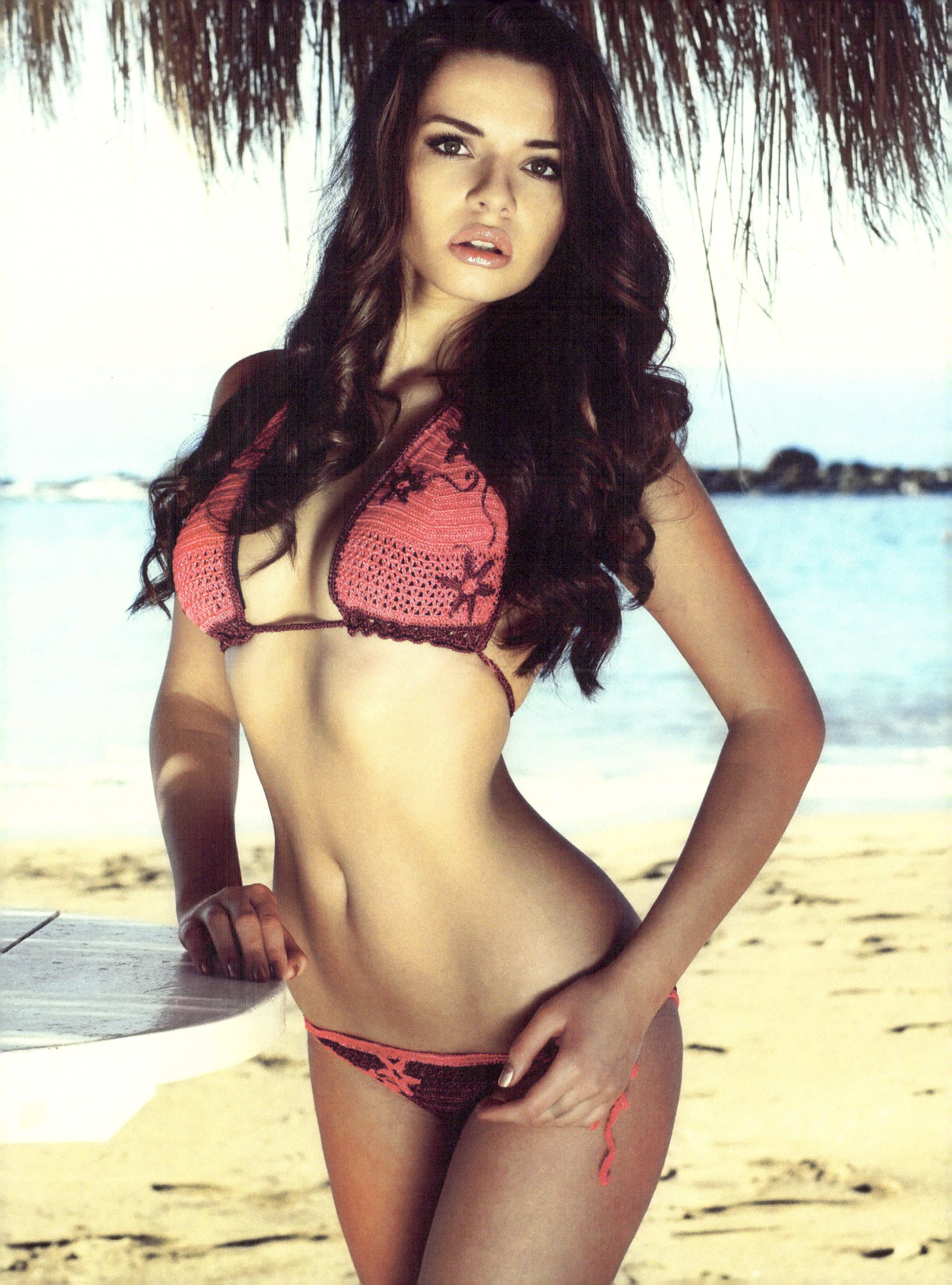

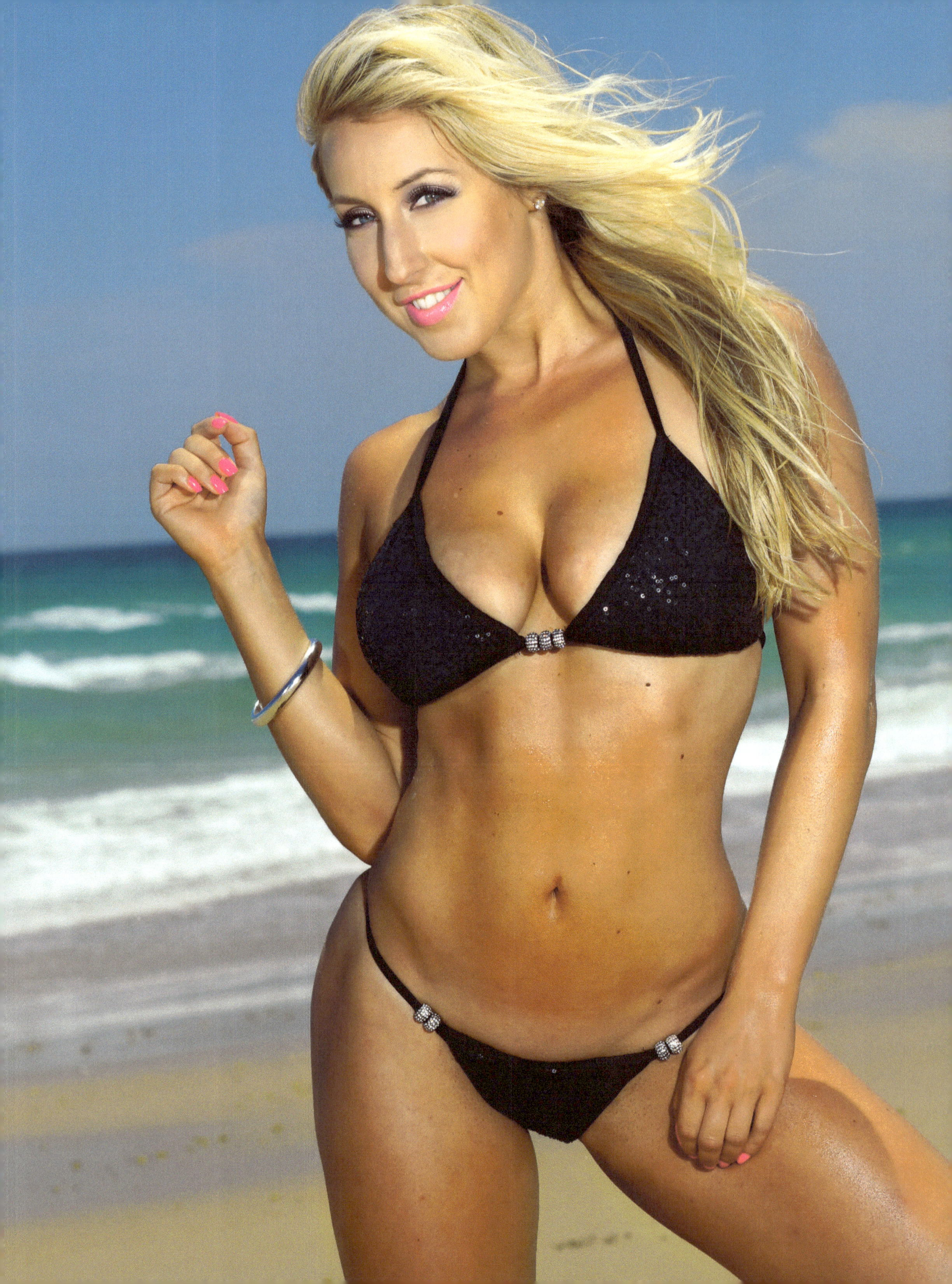

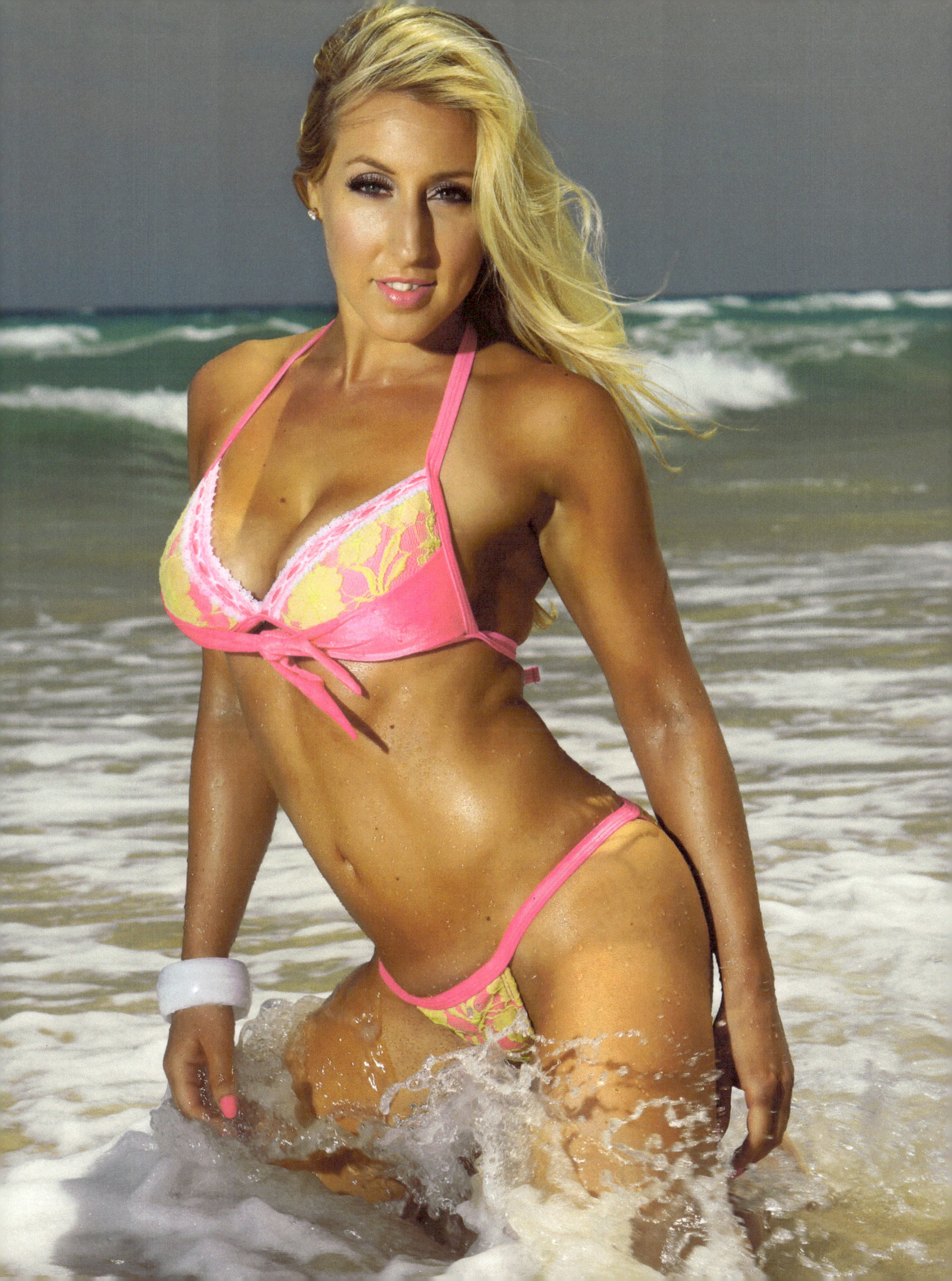

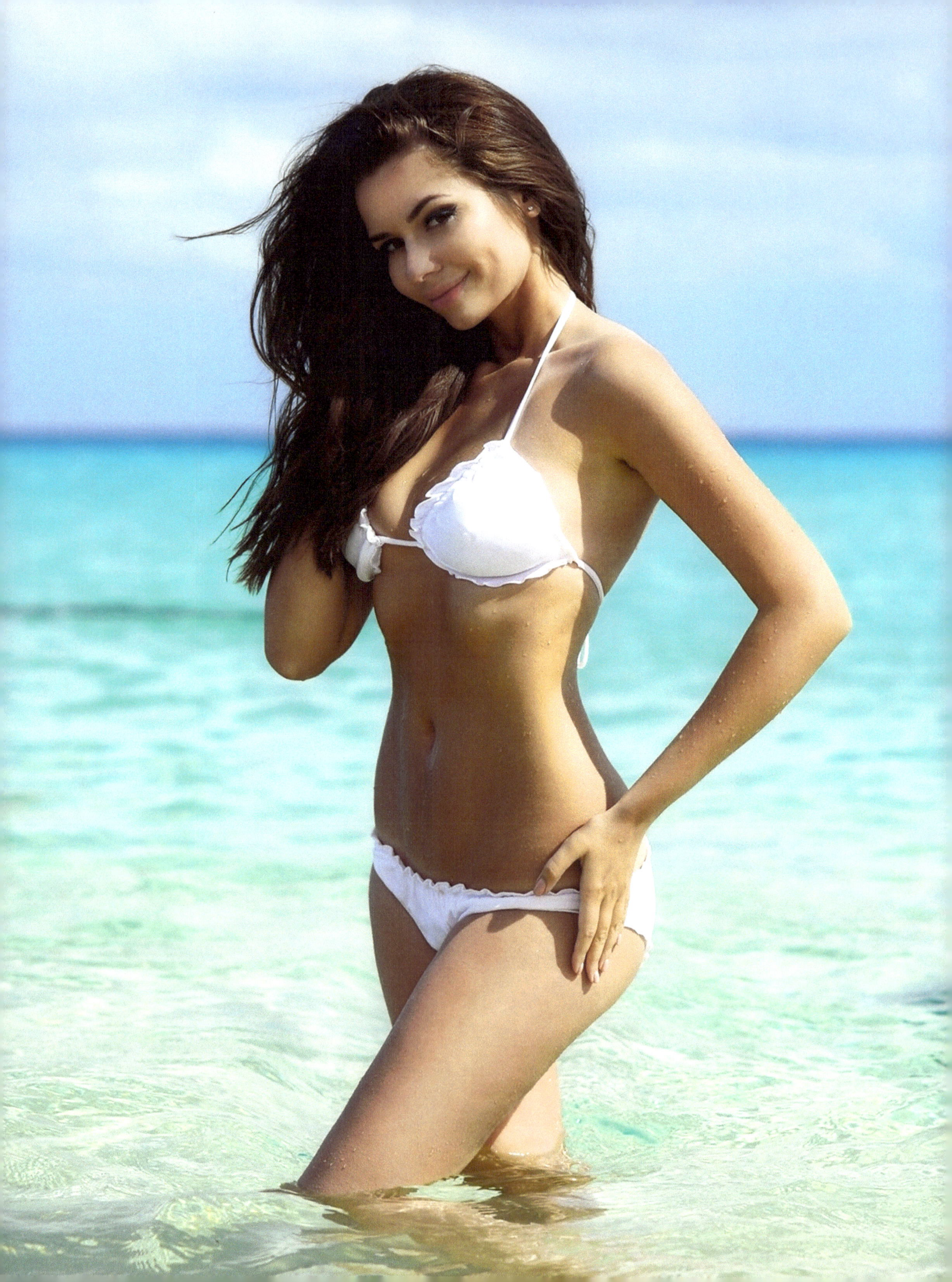

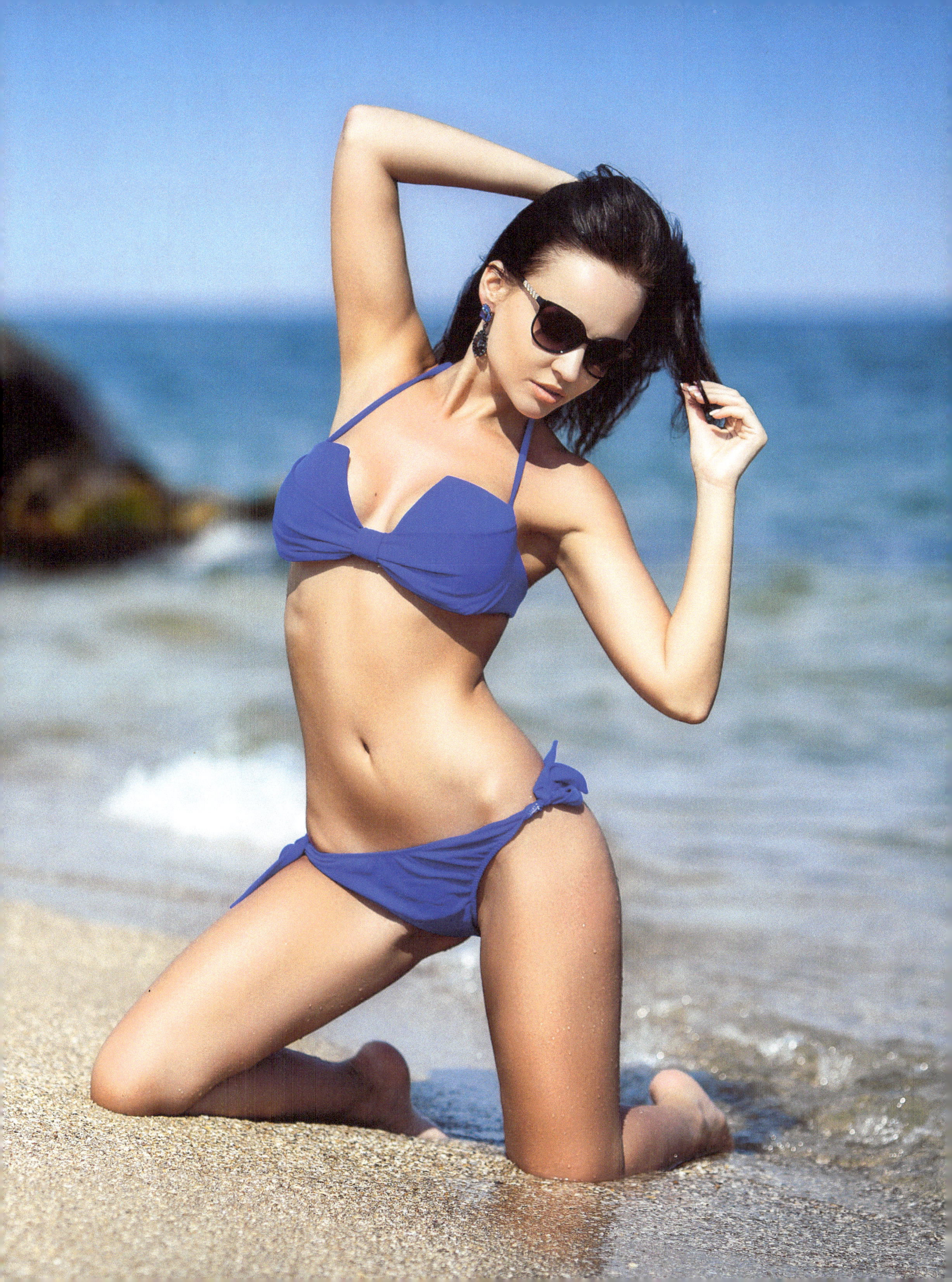

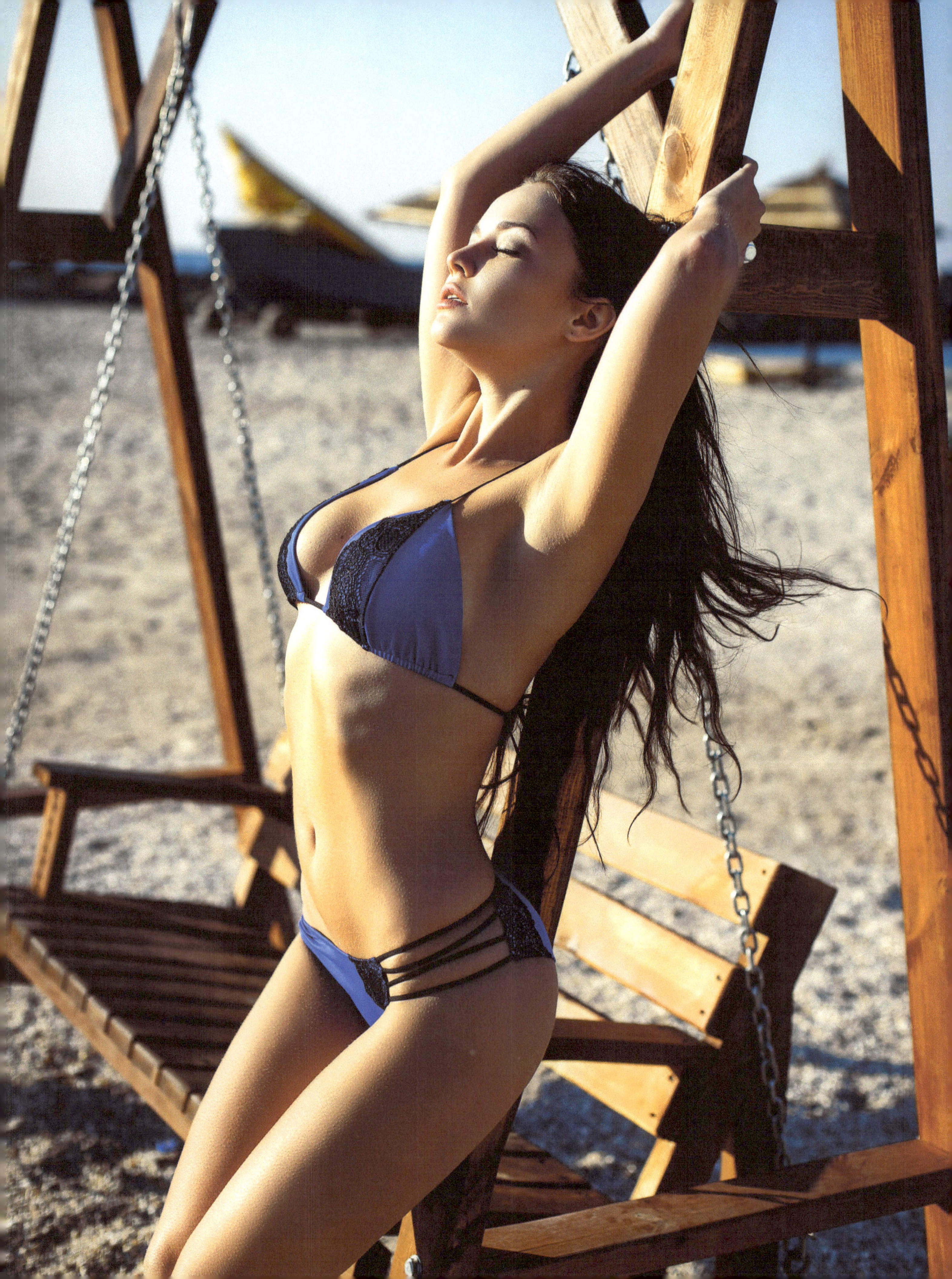

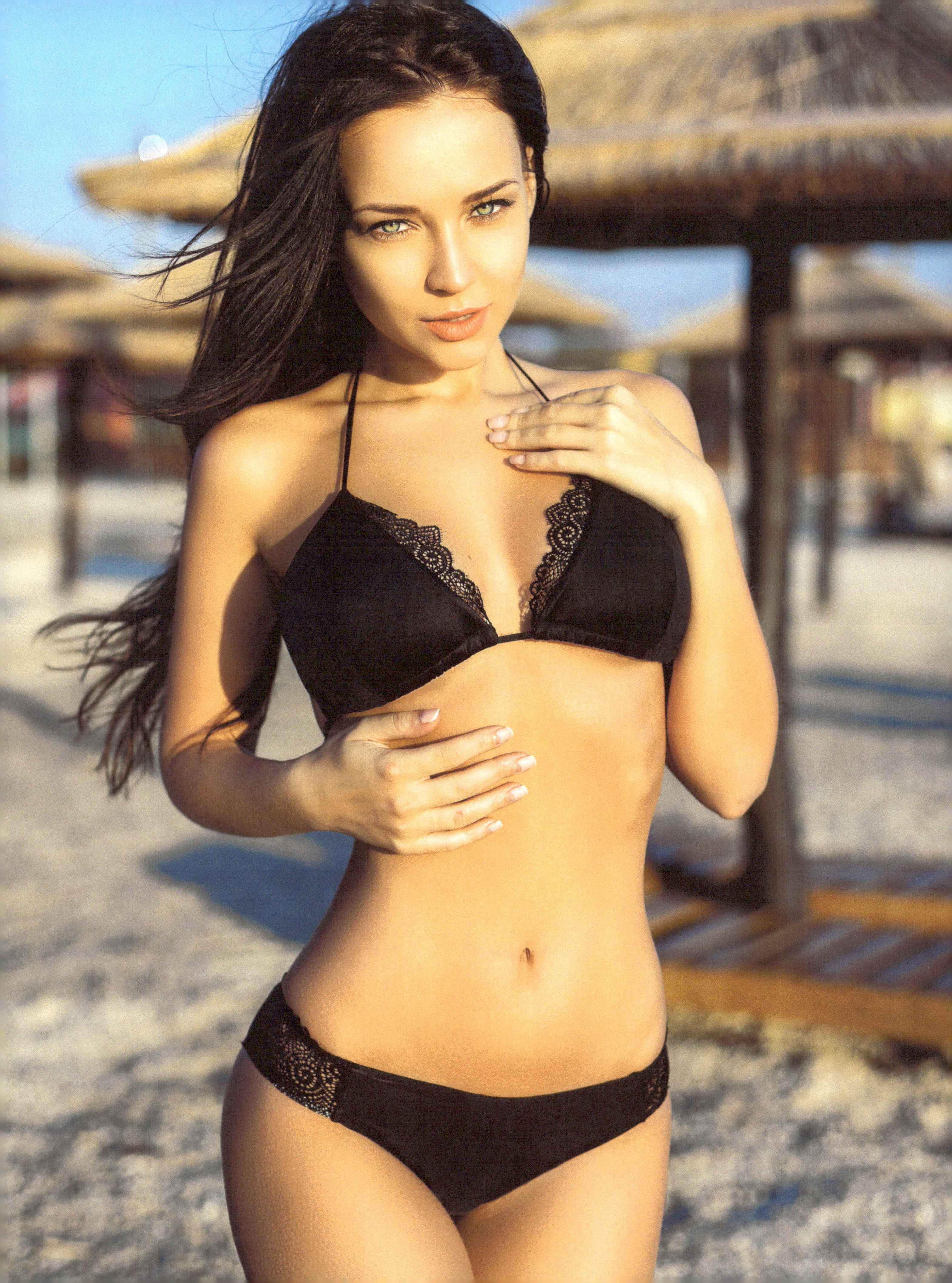

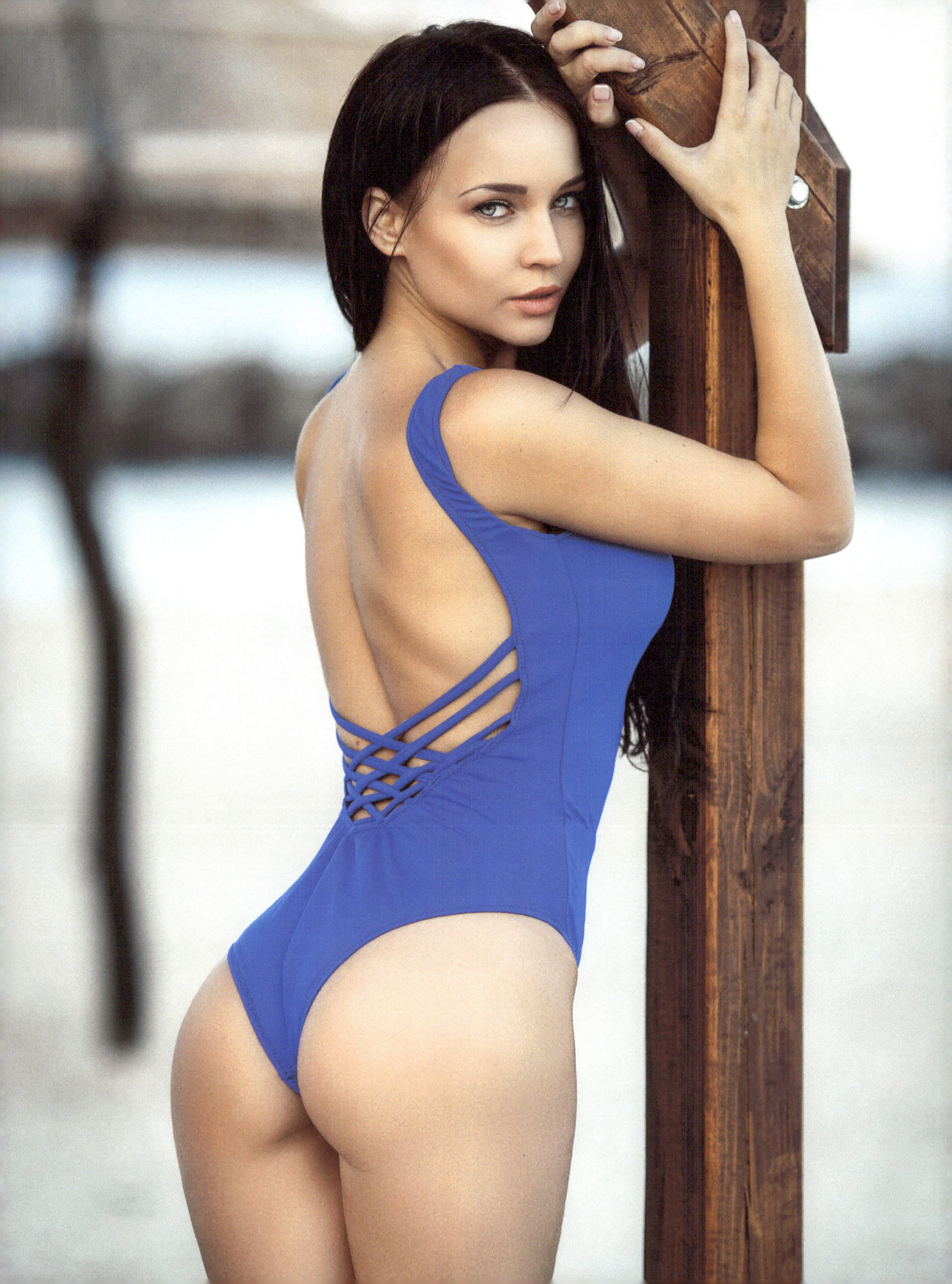

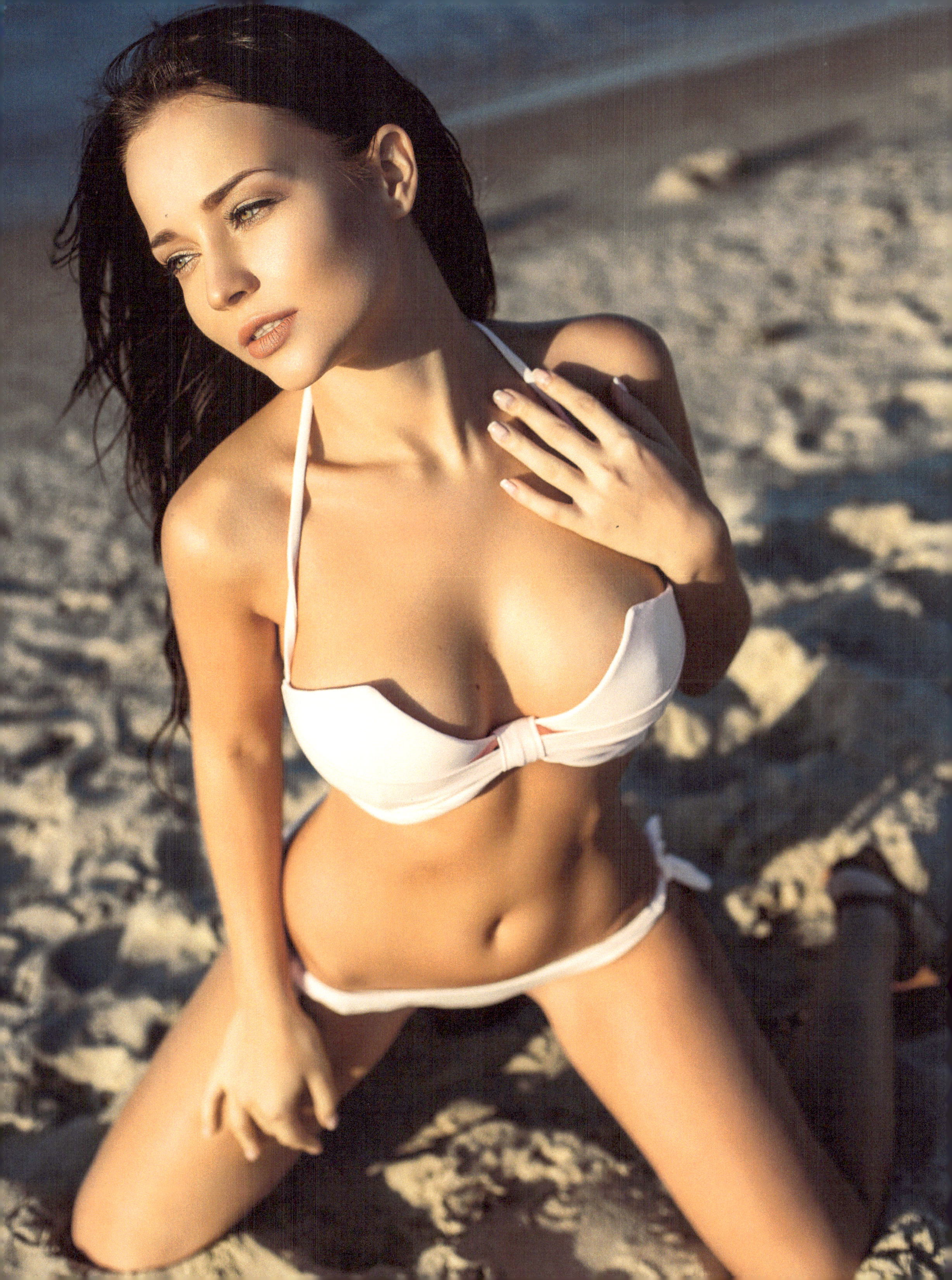

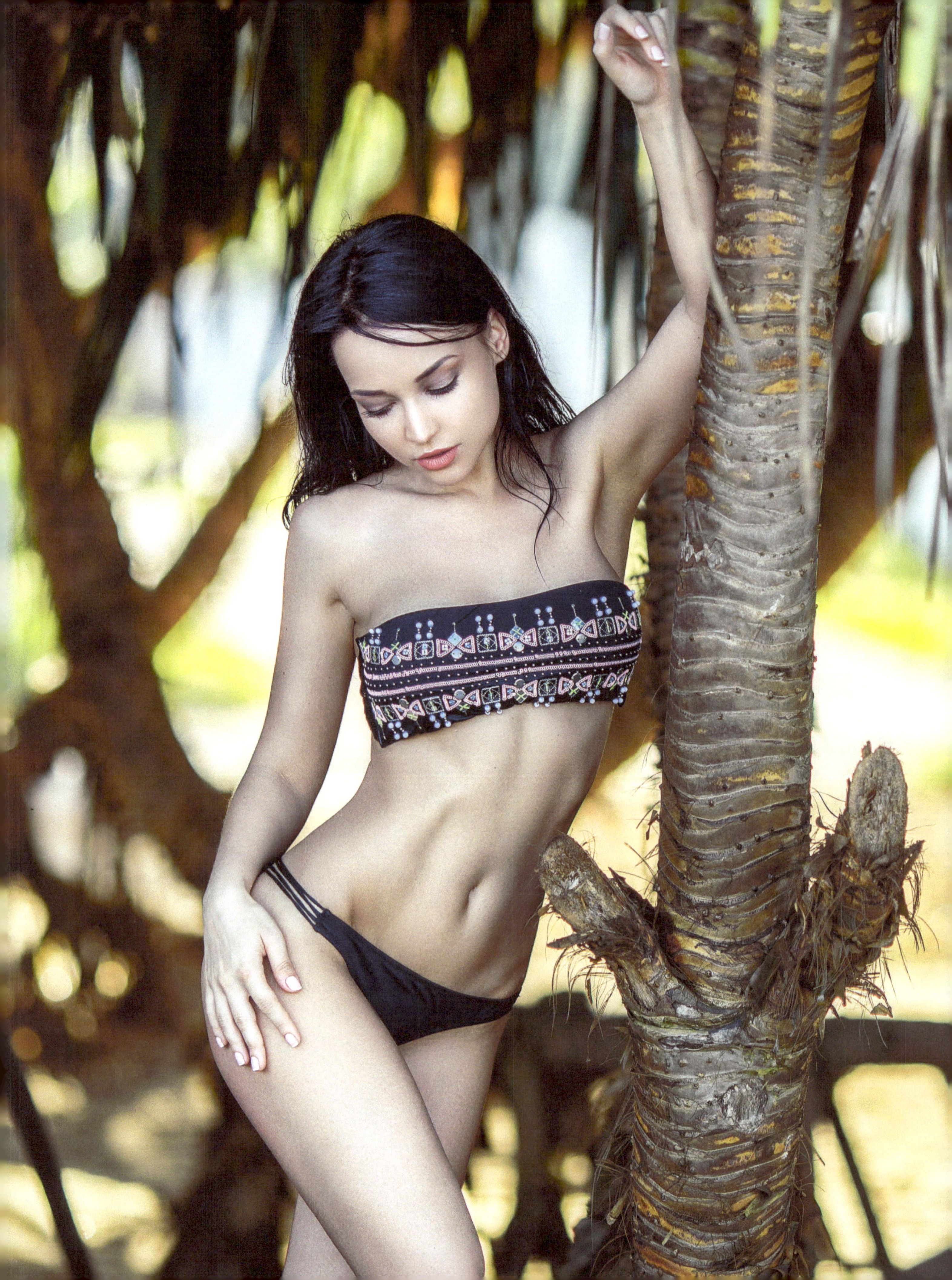

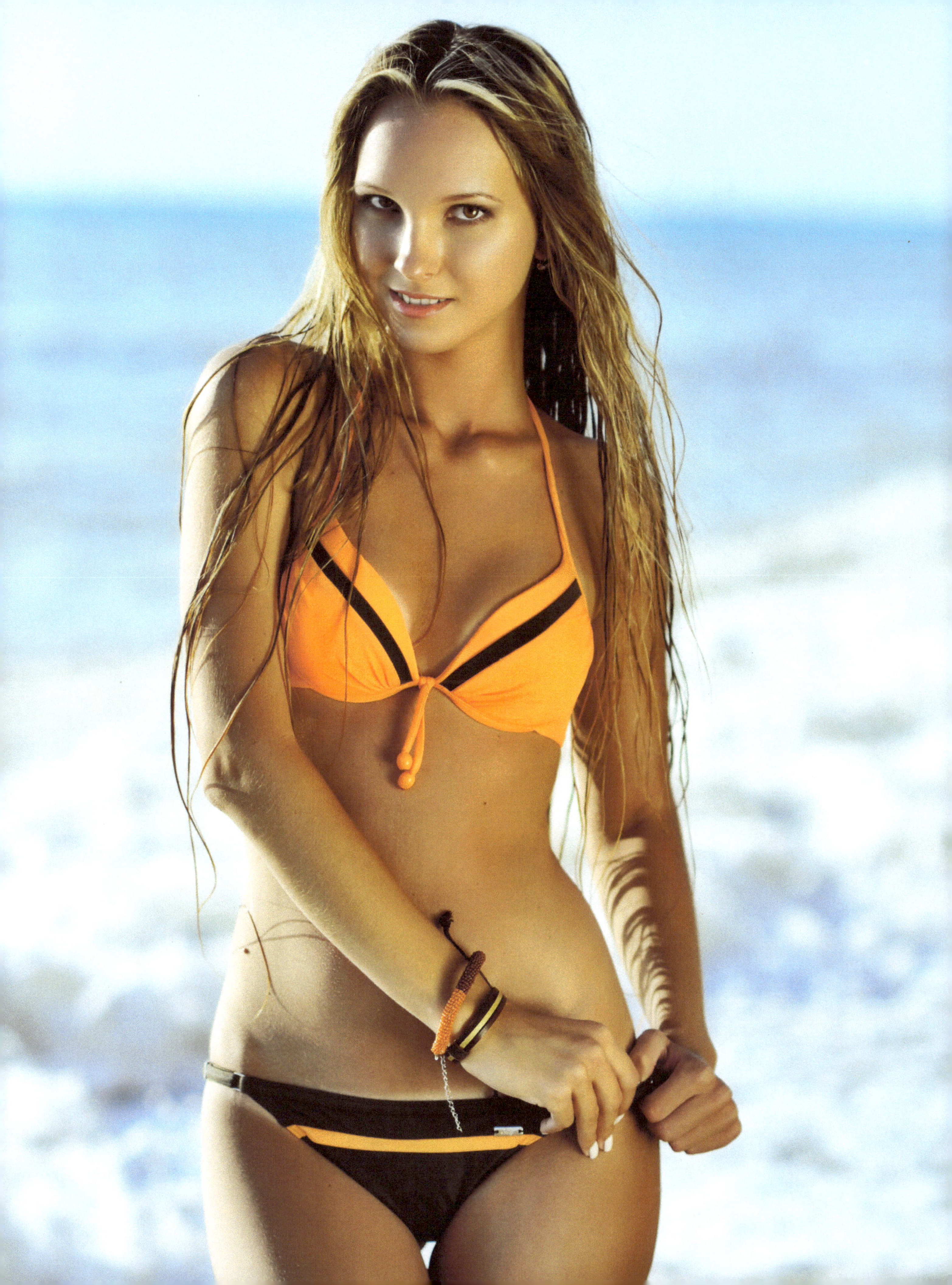

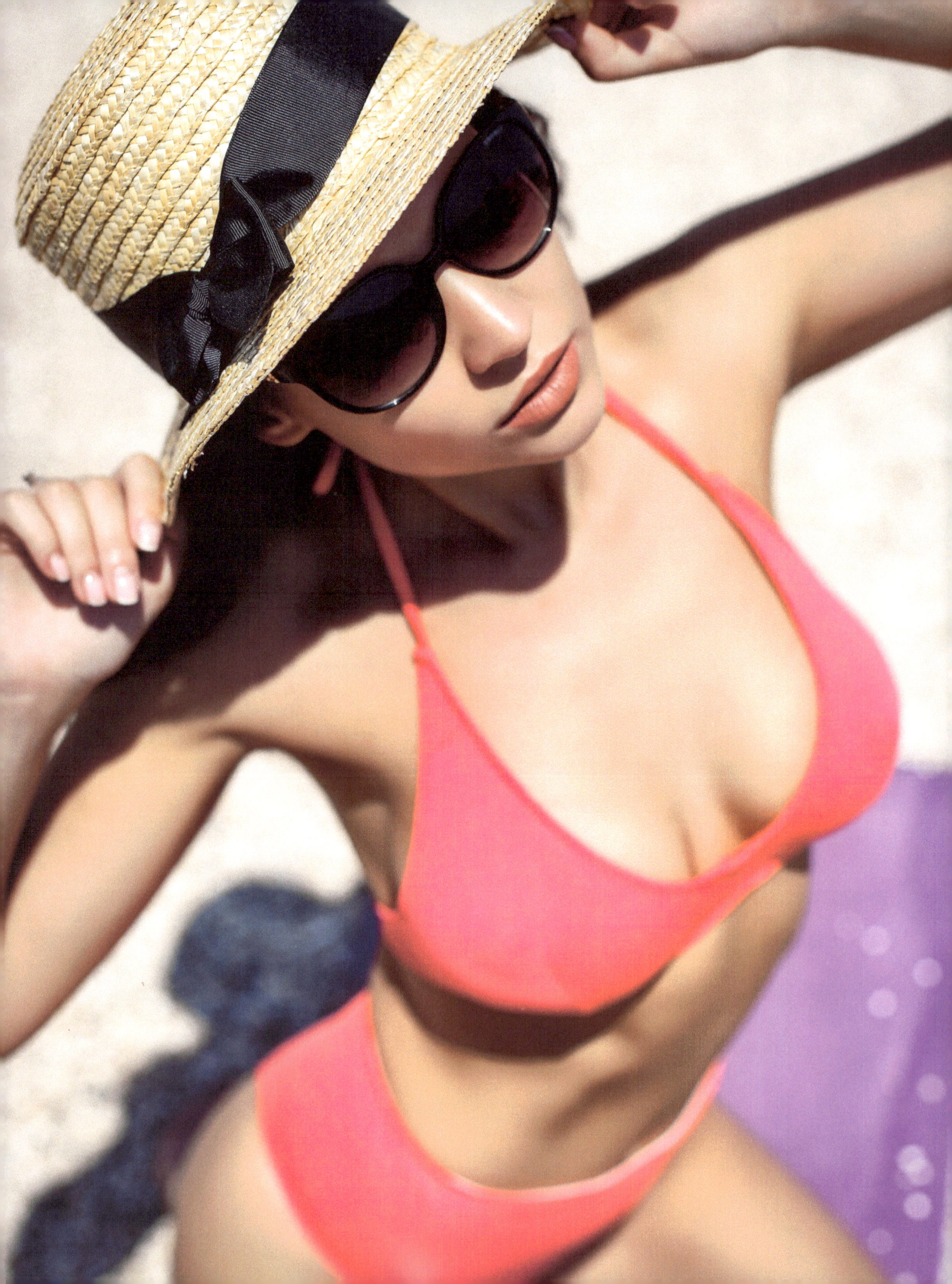

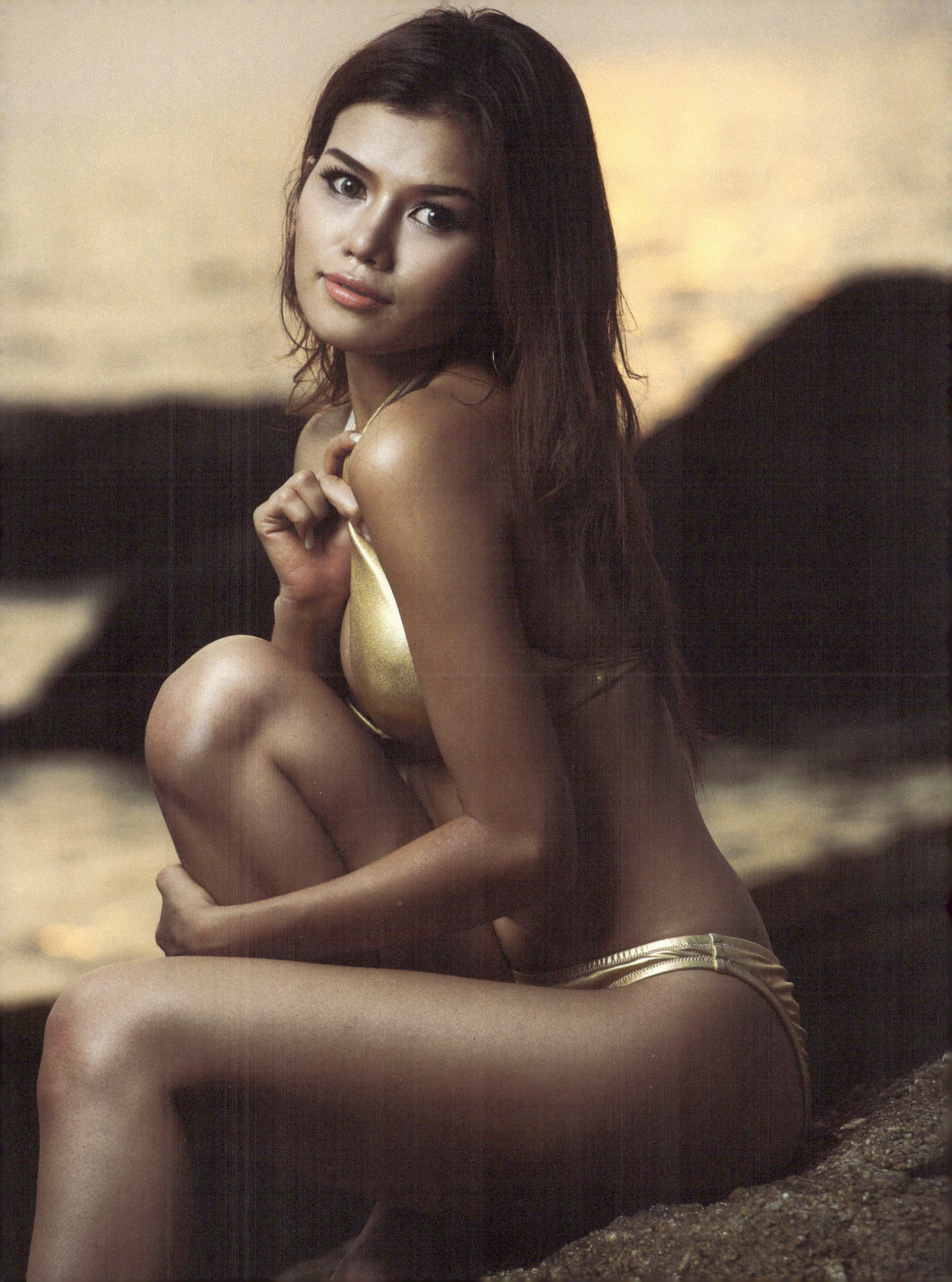

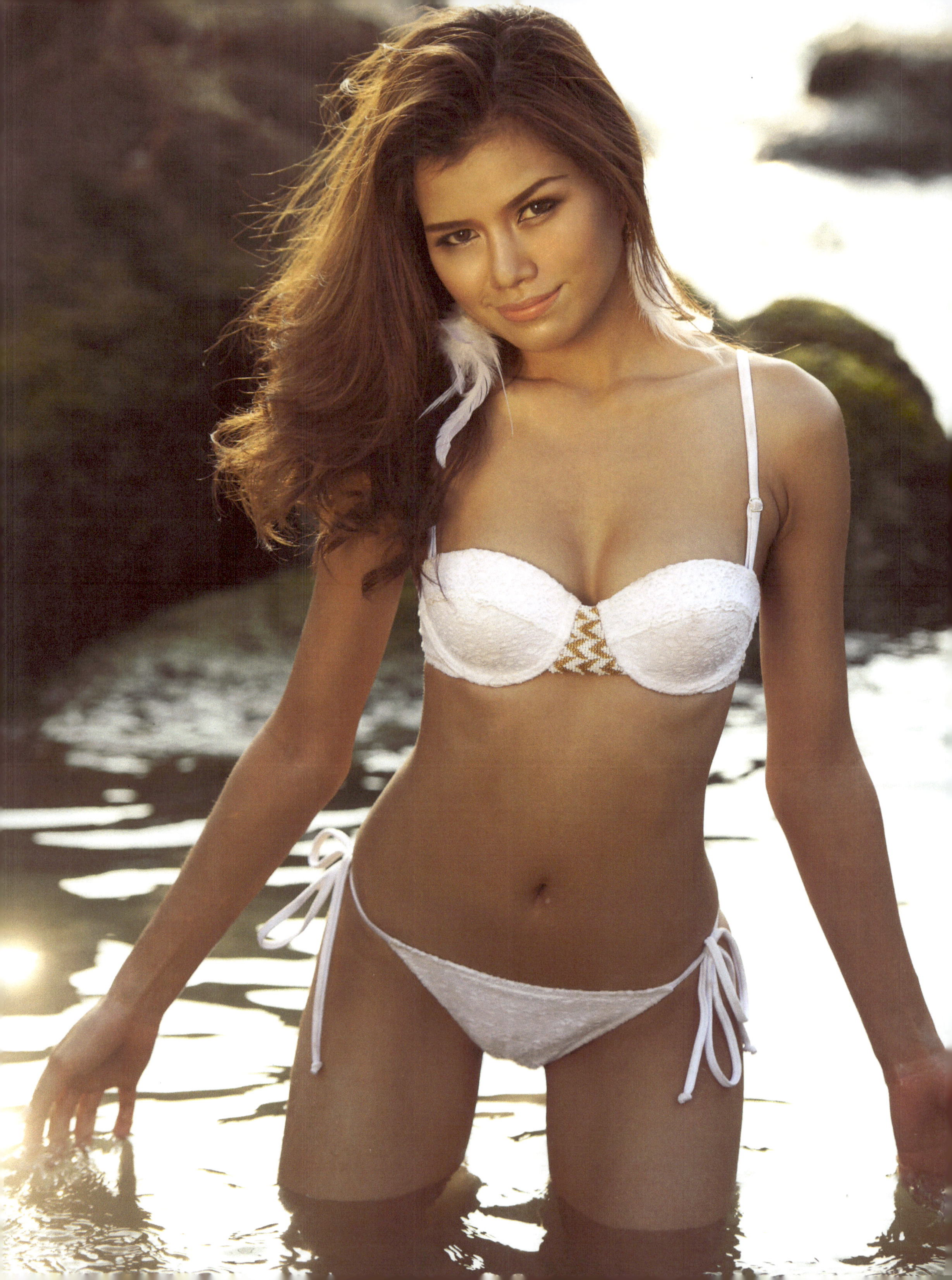

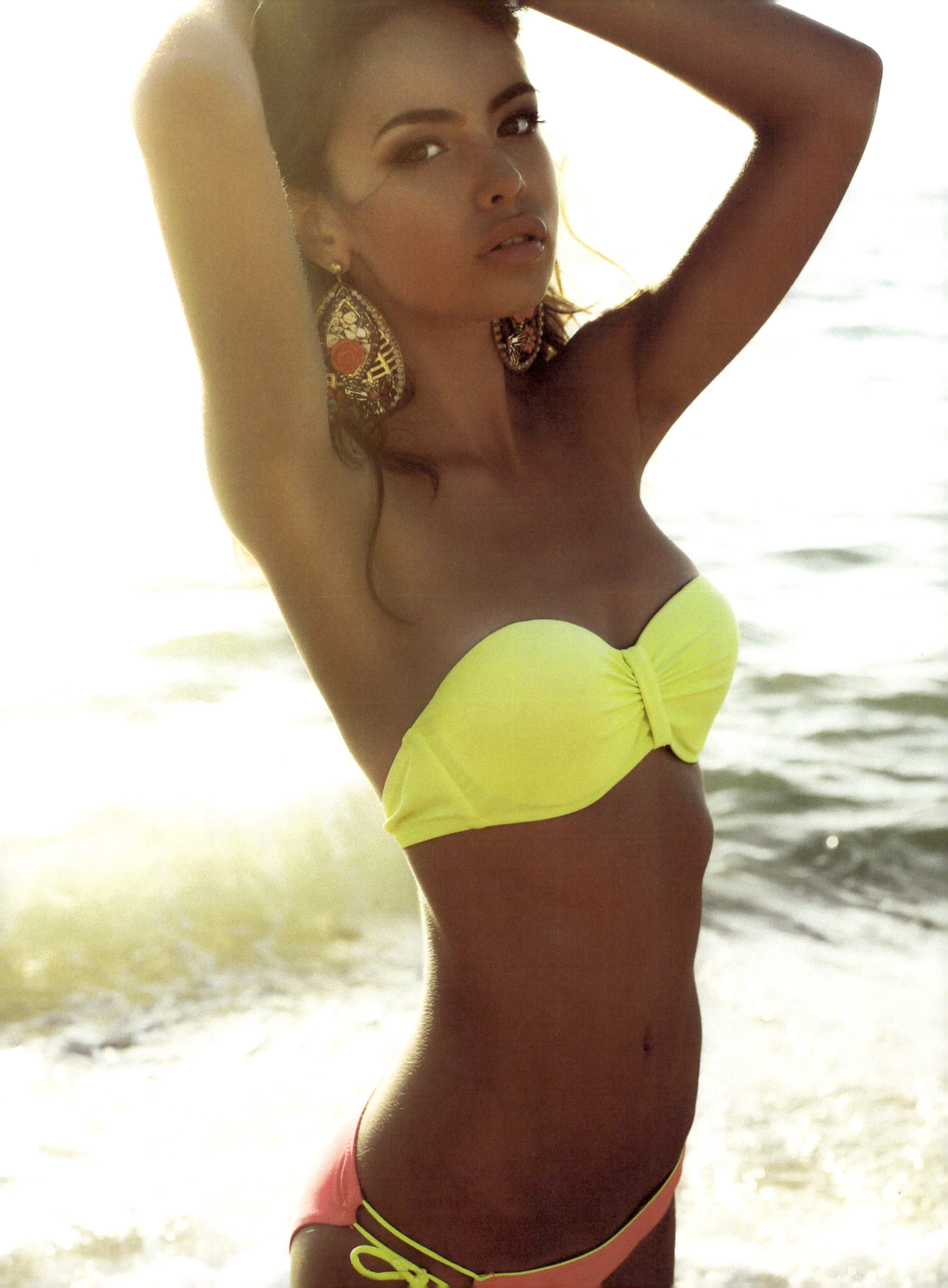

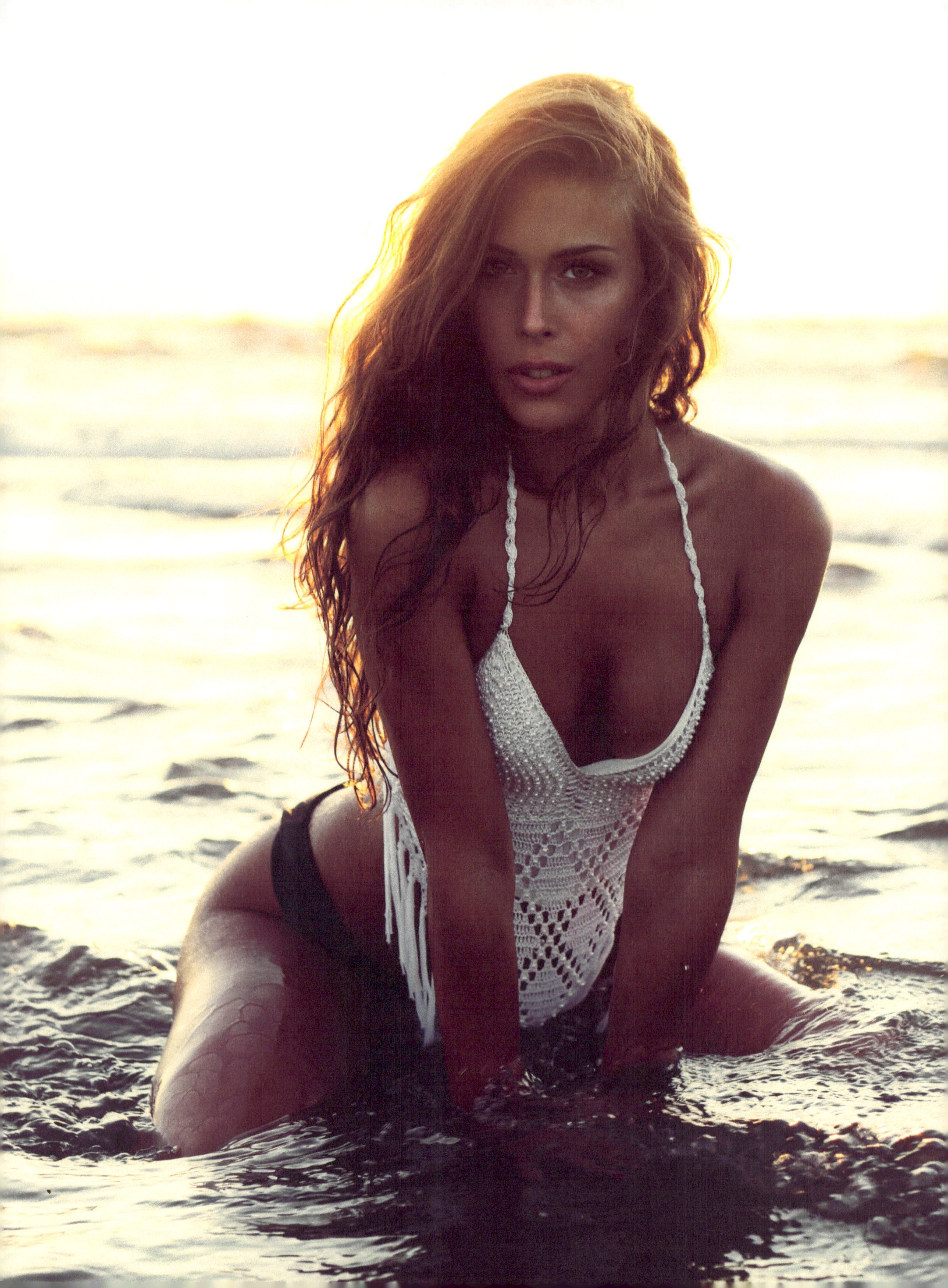

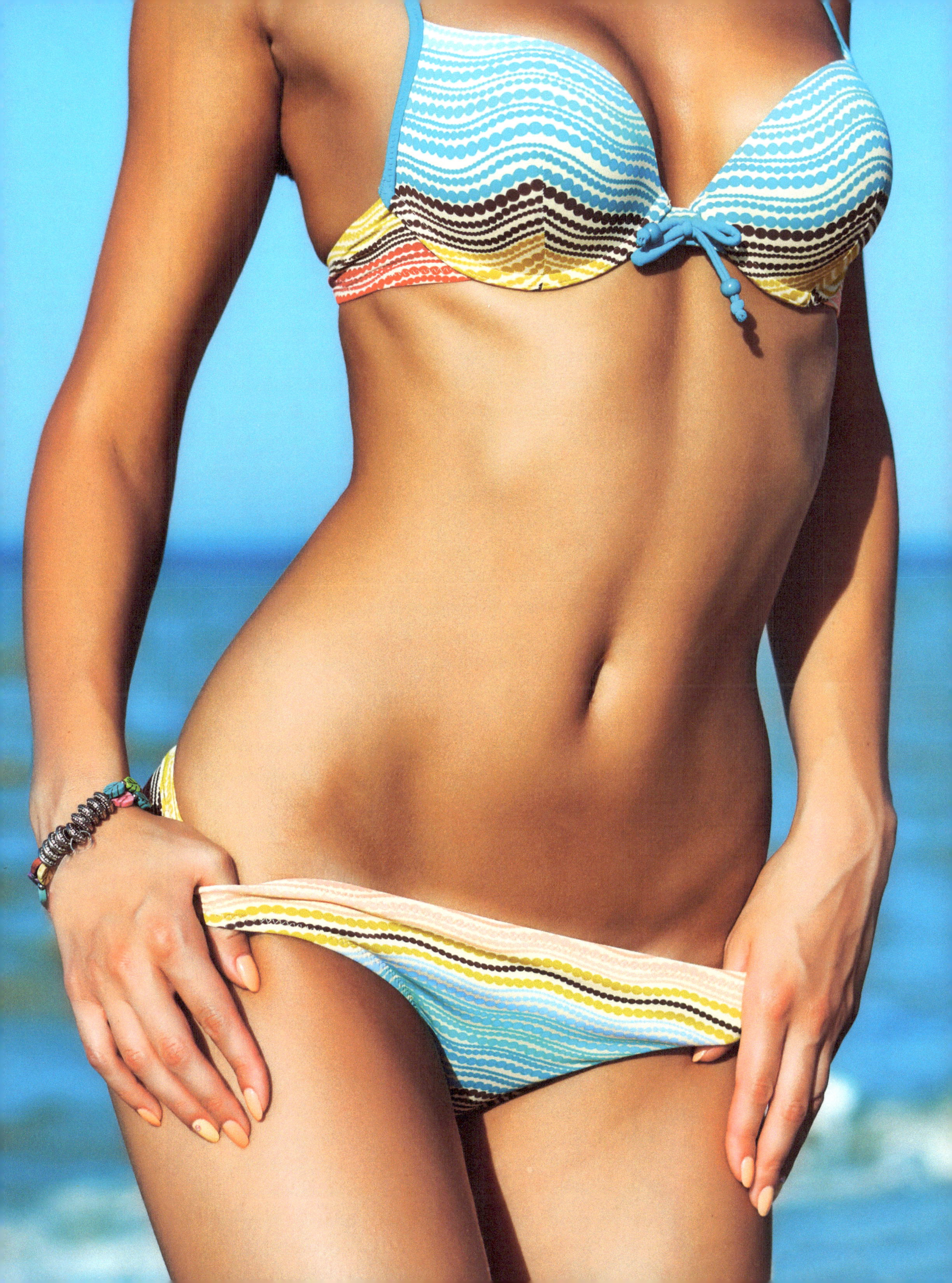

www.ingramcontent.com/pod-product-compliance
Lightning Source LLC
Chambersburg PA
CBHW050417180526
45159CB00005B/2311
* 9 7 8 1 5 3 9 6 1 3 5 5 8 *